This Book is a

Gift

from

....

to

....

on the occasion of

....

date

....

The

MYSTERY

of

SLEEP

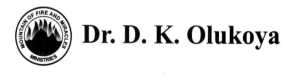 **Dr. D. K. Olukoya**

© 2012 AD - THE MYSTERY OF SLEEP
DR. D. K. OLUKOYA

ISBN: 978-978-920-063-4

A Publication of
**Mountain of Fire and Miracles Ministries
Press House
13, Olasimbo Street, off Olumo Road,
(By Unilag 2nd Gate), Onike, Iwaya,
P. O. Box 2990, Sabo, Yaba, Lagos, Nigeria.
☎ 0709-505-0462.
Email: mfmpresshouse@yahoo.com
Website: www.mfmpressbookstores.org**

All Scripture quotation is from the
King James Version of the Bible

Cover page illustration: Pastor (Mrs.) Shade Olukoya

First Edition - December, 2012

CONTENTS

Chapter One

THE
MYSTERY OF
SLEEP

"But while men slept, his enemy came and sowed tares, among the wheat, and went his Way."

Matthew 13:25

THE MYSTERY OF SLEEP

Sometime ago, a friend of mine boarded a vehicle to Lagos, Nigeria from the Eastern part of the country. He sat beside the driver and as they were going, he noticed that the driver was dozing. He told him to park the vehicle and sleep for a while before continuing the journey to avoid an accident, but the driver abused him and lied that he was not sleeping. Soon he dozed off again and before they knew it, they ended up in a pit. The accident occurred because the driver was sleeping but did not admit he was doing so, like many people would do. Likewise, some people allow the spirit of slumber to operate in their spiritual life.

I read the story of a man who died at the age of 75. He spent almost 25 years sleeping and only about six months to pray out of the 75 years. It is clear that the fellow had gone to hell fire. He spent one-third of his life sleeping. If you are still caged by the bed, then you cannot make any headway spiritually. The major spiritual battles that many people won in their lives were won after midnight.

 "But while men slept, his enemy came and sowed tares, among the wheat, and went his way." Matthew 13:25

The enemy does not come to entertain. Sometimes, we start firing at the enemy when he had already planted his evil seed and gone his way. We start firing when the destruction had already been done.

In the spiritual realm, there is something referred to as the mystery of the bed. The bed is a bridge between life and death. One of the places that man suffers his major defeat is on the bed. The sudden trouble of a lot of people started on their beds. One wonderful thing you can ask God to do for you in life is to give you power over the battle of the bed. When you win that battle, you will start moving the way God wants you to move. You cannot become a prayer warrior if you are still in bondage to the bed. You will not be useful to the Almighty if the bed is still your cell. You will not become anything powerful to the Almighty if you spend too long a time on your bed.

When you lose the battle of the bed, you lose all other battles. Satan has destroyed so many good things because of sleep. When you are addicted to sleep physically, it is bad, but it is even worse when it is transferred to the spirit man. Sleep gives the enemy a chance to sow tares. While men sleep, many human tragedies occur. For example, fire, hurricane and tornados sweeping homes and cities away strike sometimes before the victims wake up. So, the sleep hour is a time of insecurity and you cannot protect yourself at that time. It is a time of inactivity and a time of delusion when you assume that all is right only for you to wake up to see a great change. So, we need to be aware of the dangers of spiritual slumber as great damages may occur during this time, for the enemy is usually at work then.

Witches and powers of darkness look at many of us in amazement because they don't sleep. They don't need coffee to remain awake. I know of a fellow, a child of the devil who decided to hold vigil against a person for one month. From midnight to 3:00 a.m., he was cursing the man. However, the person being cursed was busy sleeping until he started seeing himself walking into a coffin.

At this juncture, I would like you to pray like this: You the powers of the night, my life is not your candidate, die in the name of Jesus.

If you are the kind of person who sleeps so heavily that you cannot wake up at the first tap, you need deliverance because; it means you are going deep down to the level that anything could happen to your spirit man. If your spirit man can sleep that deep, then there is a problem.

"And that knowing the time, that now it is high time to awake out of sleep: for now is our salvation nearer than when we believed." Romans 13:11

Paul said they were sleeping and had to wake up. If physical slumber is very bad, what about spiritual sleep?

Sleep is a period of rest during which the sleeper loses consciousness of his surroundings. So, the danger in sleep is the loss of awareness. The elder brother of sleep is what medical people call "coma." Some people are in "spiritual coma." Messages and prayers do not mean anything to them. They may be in church service but would not hear what the preacher is saying because they are already dead spiritually, although they are alive physically.

When a person falls asleep, all his physical activities decreases; his muscles relax and he could have a nightmare. Occasionally, a person sleep-walks. A person who is sleep-walking can rise up, go to the kitchen, drink something, go back to the bed and continue to sleep and if you say, "Who drank this thing?" He would say, "I never stood up, I did not go there." This is not common in Africa though. I pray that it will not happen to you, in Jesus' name.

Some people even discuss in their sleep. That is why a local proverb says that "sleep is the friend of death." It is during sleep that the agents of Satan in our environment lay evil eggs in peoples' lives and they try to make sure that their victims do not know what they have done because if they knew, they will shake off the evil eggs. That is why the Bible says that while men slept, his enemy came quietly, planted evil and went away. It is not all enemies that will attack you directly. In fact, most enemies will not attack you directly. They just come, lay their evil eggs and go away.

Some people would say: "When I went to sleep last night, I was okay but by the time I woke up, I had become another person." Some people go to bed sound only to wake up mad. The powers of the night waited for them to sleep and planted things in their lives.

 Please, take this prayer point: Every seed of the power of the night, roast! in the name of Jesus.

THE
SPIRITUAL
SLEEP

66 Wherefore he saith, Awake thou that sleepest, and arise from the dead, and Christ shall give thee light. **99**

Ephesians 5:14

Chapter Two

THE SPIRITUAL SLEEP

*T*here are two types of sleep: physical and spiritual sleep. In this chapter, we shall lay emphasis on spiritual sleep. The Bible categorises spiritual sleep into many classes. We shall look at some of them. This will help you to know whether you are awake or not. The fact that somebody's eyes are open does not mean that he is not sleeping spiritually.

THE SLEEP OF JONAH

"Then the mariners were afraid, and cried every man unto his god, and cast forth the wares that were in the ship into the sea, to

lighten it of them. But Jonah was gone down into the sides of the ship; and he lay, and was fast asleep. So the shipmaster came to him, and said unto him, What meanest thou, O sleeper? Arise, call upon thy God, if so be that God will think upon us, that we perish not." Jonah 1:5-6

CHARACTERISTICS OF JONAH'S SLEEP

It was an unrealistic sleep, a sleep of illusion. The storm was raging, men were in danger, but Jonah did not realise it at all. Likewise, many people today think that they can put a cover over their heads and all the bad things they are seeing around them would just go away simply because they are sleeping. No, they will not go away. The sailor confronted Jonah: **"What meanest thou, O sleeper arise, call upon thy God. Can't you see what is happening around?"**

There are many people like Jonah, a lot of things are happening around them, yet they are sleeping. Many today are roaming about sleeping unrealistically. Their sin is raging like the hurricane and it's as dark as the night and the danger is great, but they want to believe that everything is going to be all right. That is why Paul warns: **"Awake thou that sleepest and arise from the dead and the light of Christ shall shine upon thee."**

Unfortunately, many will die under this delusion because their eyes are covered, they think that the world will just go on like that and that nothing will happen. They believe that politicians will be politicians, military men will be military men, governors will be governors, etc. No! Very soon, things will happen. If you are sleeping like Jonah, I pray that the Lord will deliver you, in Jesus' name.

Some people have the call of God upon their lives and God has told them where to go, but they have slept off like Jonah and have also decided to go another way. God told Jonah to go to Nineveh but he headed for Tarshish and slept off on the way. Eventually, he went from his bed of sleep into the mouth of a fish and was there for three days. He did three days dry fast in the belly of the fish because of unrealistic sleep. He was running away from God and consoled himself by sleeping.

THE SLEEP OF THE APOSTLE AND
THE SLEEP OF THE DISCIPLES

●————————————————————————

What is the nature of the sleep of the disciples? It is the sleep of weariness. Mark 14:37 says: **"And he cometh, and findeth them sleeping, and saith unto Peter, Simon, sleepest thou? Couldest not thou watch one hour?"** He first called him Peter and later called him Simon. There is a difference between the two names - Peter means "rock" while Simon means "reed." Anytime Peter began to do a slow motion in the Bible, Jesus would not call him Peter, He would say Simon, and when he does well, He would call him Peter.

When Peter left Jesus and began to fish after the resurrection, Jesus said: **"Simon, son of Jonah, lovest thou me..."** Here He called him Simon which means a reed, somebody who shakes here and there. **"Simon, sleepest thou? Couldest not thou watch one hour?"** That is, could you not do one hour vigil? There are many people like that. The only vigil they do effectively with minimal sleep may be the ones organised by the church. Such people are deceiving themselves.

When you cannot sit down and do a personal vigil for at least one hour, you are sleeping the sleep of the disciples. Jesus asked His disciples to pray for danger was coming. The betrayal was to come that night and soldiers were coming. Perhaps, if Peter had prayed that one hour prayer, he would not have denied the Lord. When danger came, they stood up and were wide awake but that could not help the situation. I pray that you will not wake up when it is too late, in the name of Jesus.

Today, people are exhausted and weighed down and their senses are numb spiritually. There is a need to be watchful, for the enemy will attack when we least expect. While righteous men sleep, the enemy does not sleep. The Bible says: **"Be sober, be vigilant for the devil, your adversary walketh about seeking whom he may devour."** Evil lurks in every corner when the righteous are weary. The disciples slept the sleep of weariness and we saw where it landed them.

THE SLEEP OF SAMSON

It is very sad to know that many men are sleeping the sleep of Samson. They leave their wives at home and have located a local Delilah somewhere and they are sleeping there. To worsen their case, their friends who will come and smoke cigarette at their funeral are encouraging them to die. Samson, whose birth was prophesied by an angel, a supernatural man, a superhuman, could not withstand Delilah's lap.

 "And she made him sleep upon her knees; and she called for a man, and she caused him to shave off the seven locks of his head; and she began to afflict him, and his strength went from him." Judges 16:19

The seven locks of his head stand for perfection.

WHAT IS THE NATURE OF SAMSON'S SLEEP?

It is the sleep of presumption. That is, the spirit of "I can handle it, no problem," the spirit of over-confidence. Samson knew that he was in danger for Delilah was after the secret of His power, but he could not help himself. Delilah made him to sleep on her knees and she cut off his hair. When he awoke due to the cry of the Philistines, he said: **"I will go out like other times"** , but the Bible says that he did not know that the Lord had departed from him. He was surprised that day because he had presumed that everything was still okay. Then his eyes were pulled out and he was made to grind pepper in the mill of the enemy. It is wrong to presume that you are safe and therefore place yourself in danger. One day, you may wake up and find that the Lord has departed from you.

THE SLEEP OF THE SLUGGARD

A person who wants to sit for an examination and is sleeping eight hours everyday will end up a failure.

"I went by the field of the slothful, and by the vineyard of the man void of understanding, and lo, it was all grown over with thorns, and nettles had covered the face thereof, and the stone wall thereof was

broken down. Then I saw, and considered it well. I looked upon it, and received instruction. Yet a little sleep, a little slumber, a little folding of the hands to sleep; so shall thy poverty come as one that travelleth, and they want as an armed man." Proverbs 24:30-34

THE SLEEP OF EUTYCHUS

"And upon the first day of the week, when the disciples came together to break bread, Paul preached unto them, ready to depart on the morrow; and continued his speech until midnight. And there were many lights in the upper chamber, where they were gathered together. And there sat in a window a certain young man named Eutychus, being fallen into a deep sleep; and as Paul was long preaching, he sunk down with sleep, and fell down from the third floor, and was taken up dead. And Paul went down, and fell on him, and embracing him said, trouble not yourselves, for his life is in him. When he therefore was come up again, and had broken bread, and eaten, and talked a long while, even till break of day, so he departed. And they brought the young man alive, and were not a little comforted." Act 20:7-12

This is the longest sermon in the Bible. Here was a man who had a bed at home and could have slept at home, but he did not do so but came to the house of God and decided that everything they were saying there was sleeping tablet and he started sleeping, and as he slept, the enemy that pursued him to the meeting said, "We shall use you to disgrace them here." He slept until he fell down. If a fellow could sleep like that while a message was going on, it showed that he would not be useful at a vigil. He would be a useless disciple.

One of the things that has captured especially this country is that, there are some people who wake up in the morning to take over the whole day while believers are still snoring on their beds. The children of the bond woman give orders to the day to co-operate with them while Christians are still snoring. If you wake up at 8:00 a.m. and pray a five-minute prayer, and later you say, "I don't know how today went," that is the sleep of Eutychus.

THE SLEEP OF THE FOOLISH VIRGINS

We have their story in Matthew chapter 25. They did not have sufficient oil in their lamps yet they were sleeping.

HOW DO YOU KNOW WHETHER YOU ARE ALREADY DEEP IN SPIRITUAL SLUMBER?

1. **When prayer ceases to be a priority to you.**

2. **When you become content with the spiritual knowledge that you have already acquired.**

3. **When your biblical knowledge is not applied inwardly:** You just go to church, hear the sermon and read the Bible, but you do not apply them

inwardly. They have no effect on your thought life or on your way of life.

4. **When thoughts about heaven and eternity cease to be regular in your heart:** You don't think about heaven. It does not cross your mind that this world is not a permanent place. You are only concerned about material wealth. It is a sign of spiritual slumber. You forget that our period on earth is temporary, that very soon, all you have acquired in this world would become raw materials for fire.

5. **When services in the house of God hold no delight for you:** You are not interested in what goes on there.

6. **When spiritual discussion becomes a source of embarrassment to you:** In your office for example, talking about Jesus or spiritual things become highly embarrassing because you know that those around will certainly accuse you that you are not behaving like a Christian.

7. **When things like leisure, sport, recreation, entertainment, etc, take a larger part of your time:** Sleep has crept in and if you don't wake up, the enemy will come and sow tares or lay eggs if they have not already done so.

8. **When you commit the sin of the mind and body without your conscience pricking you.**

9. **When the aspiration for holiness is no longer paramount in your heart:** When you look for Scriptures to back up your unholy behaviours; you know the truth but you are running away from it. People can always recognise the truth when they see it and they can always know when they are trying to wriggle away from the blunt truth. The truth may be bitter and unpalatable, but it is very stubborn; no matter what you do to it, it will stand looking at you. If you knock it down, it will stand; you throw it away, it will stand; you bury it, it will come up. It may take time to manifest, but it must manifest.

10. **When acquisition of worldly materials is the major part of your thinking.**

11. **When you are paying lip service to the word of God:** Christian words just from the lips and not from the heart. Surrendering to Jesus only what is convenient for you is a sign of spiritual slumber.

12. **Taking the Lord's name in vain shows that you are sleeping:** You talk about the Lord as if He is your houseboy. Saying that He has said something when He has not spoken; saying you received a revelation when you didn't receive anything.

13. **Watching dirty movies and T.V. shows and reading impure literature is a sign that you have already slept:** A lot of people can stay glued to the T.V. for hours without sleeping, but immediately you say, "Let us pray", then they sleep off.

14. **When with the slightest excuse, you avoid spiritual duties - you have slept.**

15. **When you are contended with your lack of spiritual power and you no longer seek power from on high:** The first key to spiritual power is lack of rest in your soul and disquietness in your spirit because you are not satisfied with your present level.

16. **When you pardon your sins and your laziness by saying that God understands - you are spiritually asleep.**

17. **When you are a Christian that can easily adjust to the lifestyle of the world:** You dress differently to church and differently outside. It is a sign that you are spiritually asleep. If you still crack dirty jokes with unbelievers, or they feel at ease in your company to do whatever they like, then you are asleep. The correct stand is that they should find it very difficult to do or say certain things before you.

18. **When you are willing to cheat your employer - you have slept.**

Today, my cry to God for you is that you will wake up like

Paul admonished. Paul was not talking to unbelievers, he was talking to Christians. He said: **"Awake thou that sleepest and arise from the dead; and the light of Christ shall shine upon thee."** So, it is time to awake from our sleep because; now our salvation is nearer than it was before. Do not waste time to clear the evil eggs that the enemy has laid in your life while you were sleeping. So that the time you should be doing useful things for the Lord, you would not be busy using it to do deliverance for what happened to you while you were sleeping. It is better to be awake and pursue the enemy right into their gates. This is a serious matter and it must be tackled aggressively.

It is not a good thing to be a believer and God does not speak to you. You cannot hear Him even on simple things of life such as your job. You are a Christian, yet you are gambling with life. When somebody begins to experiment with life, he does not get the best out of it. The best thing is to be in the right place at the right time and to be sure of what the Almighty wants to do with your life. The fact that what you are doing is good does not mean it has the approval of heaven.

If you have things to sort out with the Lord, do that now. Look back at your spiritual life and look at what is happening now. Are you having the best? Haven't you noticed the mistakes that you made because you could not hear from heaven? Haven't you noticed the mistakes were because you were spiritually asleep? You have given your enemy opportunity to plant seeds. Sort yourself out with the Lord. Make a promise that as from now on, your spirit man will be on fire and that fire would forever burn on the altar of your life. Why should your ears be making noise but you are hearing nothing? Why should your eyes be itching but you are seeing nothing? You know everything about your field of specialization, but you do not know what the Holy Spirit is saying about your life.

PRAYER POINTS

1. *O Lord, wake me up from every spiritual sleep, in the name of Jesus.*

2. *Every evil seed sown into my life while I was sleeping, be removed by fire! in the name of Jesus.*

THE POWER
TO ERASE
EVIL RECORDS

" Records, whether divine or evil could be transferred or simply inherited, and it would be binding on generations Yet unborn. **"**

Chapter Three

THE POWER TO ERASE EVIL RECORDS

"Therefore thus saith the LORD concerning Jehoiakim the son of Josiah king of Judah; They shall not lament for him, saying, Ah my brother! or, Ah sister! they shall not lament for him, saying, Ah lord! or, Ah his glory! He shall be buried with the burial of an ass, drawn and cast forth beyond the gates of Jerusalem. Go up to Lebanon, and cry; and lift up thy voice in Bashan, and cry from the passages: for all thy lovers are destroyed. I spake unto thee in thy prosperity; but thou saidst, I will not hear. This hath been thy manner from thy youth, that thou obeyedst not my voice. The wind shall eat up all thy pastors, and thy lovers shall go into captivity: surely then shalt thou be ashamed and confounded for all thy wickedness. O inhabitant of Lebanon, that makest thy nest in the cedars, how gracious shalt thou be when pangs come upon thee, the pain as of a woman in travail! As I live, saith the LORD, though Coniah the son of Jehoiakim king of Judah were the signet upon my right hand, yet would I pluck thee thence; And I will give thee into the hand of them that seek thy life, and into the hand of them whose face thou fearest, even into the hand of Nebuchadrezzar king of Babylon, and into the hand of the Chaldeans. And I will cast thee out, and thy mother that bare thee, into another country, where ye were not born; and there shall ye die. But to the land whereunto they desire to return, thither shall they not return. Is this man Coniah a despised broken idol? is he a vessel wherein is no pleasure? wherefore are they cast out, he and his seed, and are cast into a land which they know not? O earth, earth, earth, hear the word of the LORD. Thus saith the LORD, Write ye this man childless, a man that shall not prosper in his days: for no man of his seed shall prosper, sitting upon the throne of David, and ruling any more in Judah." Jeremiah 22:18-30

*T*here are evil records which must be erased. Many people are busy suffering from recorded evil messages. What does is mean to record?

The simple dictionary meaning of a record is to set down for preservation in writing or other permanent form.

SPIRITUAL RECORDS

To record is to register. There are physical records such as we have on papers and other materials, and there are also non-physical records. An example of physical record as found in the Bible is in Exodus 17: 13-14.

God gave an instruction to Moses to record an event of war that took place between the children of Israel and the Amalekikes. The defeat of Amalek through the prayer of Moses and the sword of Joshua was ordered to be recorded for a memorial in a book. This of course is a physical record, but also generated a record in the realm of the spirit.

"And Joshua discomfited Amalek and his people with the edge of the sword. And the LORD said unto Moses, Write this for a memorial in a book, and rehearse it in the ears of Joshua: for I will utterly put out the remembrance of Amalek from under heaven." Exodus 17:13-14

The non-physical records otherwise known as invisible records are records that cannot be seen with our physical eyes. They are there because pronouncements were made and such pronouncements were recorded as invisible records by some materials. As recordings are made on paper or other materials for physical records, the non-physical records have materials which contain their recordings. Such materials include the earth, the sun, the moon, the stars, the bodies of water and so on.

An example of such records as found in the Bible is in Joshua 24:26-27:

 "And Joshua wrote these words in the book of the law of God, and took a great stone, and set it up there under an oak, that was by the sanctuary of the LORD. And Joshua said unto all the people, Behold, this stone shall be a witness unto us; for it hath heard all the words of the LORD which he spoke unto us: it shall be therefore a witness unto you, lest ye deny your God."

Here we have both physical and non-physical records. The physical record was on paper, in the Book containing the law of God, and the non-physical record was inside the stone set up under an oak tree.

NON-PHYSICAL RECORDS

Just as physical records could be good or bad, the non-physical records too could be divine or evil. An example of non-physical record is found in Deuteronomy 30:15-19:

"See, I have set before thee this day life and good, and death and evil; In that I command thee this day to love the LORD thy God, to walk in his ways, and to keep his commandments and his statutes and his judgments, that thou mayest live and multiply: and the LORD thy God shall bless thee in the land whither thou goest to possess it. But if thine heart turn away, so that thou wilt not hear, but shalt be drawn away, and worship other gods, and serve them; I denounce unto you this day, that ye shall surely perish, and that ye shall not prolong your days upon the land, whither thou passest over Jordan to go to possess it. I call heaven and earth to record this day against you, that I have set before you life and death, blessing and cursing: therefore choose life, that both thou and thy seed may live:"

REGISTERED BLESSINGS OR CURSES

Moses here is registering his pronouncements on earth and in heaven and it was binding on all the Israelites living then and generations to come, for earth and heaven heard him. From the above, it shows that an individual can register blessings or curses on earth or in heaven against another individual, or community or a race and heaven and earth will hold it. Now, the effectiveness of the blessings or curses against its targeted entity(ies) depends upon a number of factors:

1. **The spiritual strength or power of the entity(ies) or individual(s) pronouncing what is to be registered.**

2. **Whether the targeted entity(ies) is qualified for such blessing or cursing.**

When divine judgment comes upon an individual or a community, a tribe or a race, a city or a country, or even a continent because of abominations committed, an evil record will be set down against such. Hear Moses again in Deuteronomy 31:28:

 "Gather unto me all the elders of your tribes, and your officers, that I may speak these words in their ears, and call heaven and earth to record against them."

Now, see the manner in which he registered his pronouncement unto heaven and earth in Deuteronomy 32:1:

 "Give ear, O ye heavens, and I will speak; and hear, O earth, the words of my mouth."

DIVINE RECORDS

There is a divine record concerning new heaven and new earth- Revelation 21:5-6...16:

"And he that sat upon the throne said, Behold, I make all things new. And he said unto me, Write: for these words are true and faithful. And he said unto me, It is done. I am Alpha and Omega, the beginning and the end. I will give unto him that is a thirst of the fountain of the water of life freely...And the city lieth foursquare, and the length is as large as the breadth: and he measured the city with the reed, twelve thousand furlongs. The length and the breadth and the height of it are equal."

INHERITED RECORD

Records, whether divine or evil will have attached to them, a set time, a period, a season or a set cycle. The agenda of such records are to build or to destroy; to lift up or to cast down; to make to excel or to make to fail; to move forward or to make stagnant; to have a glorious destiny or a perverted destiny; to bless or to curse.

Divine records generate divine programming or divine

pull towards achieving that which had been recorded. Also, evil records generate evil programming or pull towards achieving that which had been recorded.

Records whether divine or evil could be transferred or simply inherited, and it would be binding on generations yet unborn. There was a divine record concerning what will happen to the seed of Abraham in a strange land. That record had a time factor attached to it.

 "And he said unto Abram, Know of a surety that thy seed shall be a stranger in a land that is not theirs, and shall serve them; and they shall afflict them four hundred years;" Genesis 15:13

This message came to Abram when Isaac was not yet born, but it was recorded and everything in heaven and on earth that will make this to come to pass immediately were set in motion.

There was a record concerning the rebuilding of the city

of Jericho when Joshua made a pronouncement upon it-
Joshua 6:26:

"And Joshua adjured them at that time, saying, Cursed be the man before the LORD, that riseth up and buildeth this city Jericho: he shall lay the foundation thereof in his firstborn, and in his youngest son shall he set up the gates of it."

Joshua spoke to that city and the city heard him and recorded it and Hiel tried to rebuild the city and that which was recorded happened to him in exact manner.

"In his days did Hiel the Bethelite build Jericho: he laid the foundation thereof in Abiram his firstborn, and set up the gates thereof in his youngest son Segub, according to the word of the LORD, which he spoke by Joshua the son of Nun." 1 Kings 16:34

EVIL RECORDS

Now, let us look into a very strong case of evil record concerning a particular lineage in Israel.

"**Therefore thus saith the LORD concerning Jehoiakim the son of Josiah king of Judah; They shall not lament for him, saying, Ah my brother! or, Ah sister! they shall not lament for him, saying, Ah lord! or, Ah his glory! He shall be buried with the burial of an ass, drawn and cast forth beyond the gates of Jerusalem. Go up to Lebanon, and cry; and lift up thy voice in Bashan, and cry from the passages: for all thy lovers are destroyed. I spake unto thee in thy prosperity; but thou saidst, I will not hear. This hath been thy manner from thy youth, that thou obeyedst not my voice. The wind shall eat up all thy pastors, and thy lovers shall go into captivity: surely then shalt thou be ashamed and confounded for all thy wickedness. O inhabitant of Lebanon, that makest thy nest in the cedars, how gracious shalt thou be**

when pangs come upon thee, the pain as of a woman in travail! As I live, saith the LORD, though Coniah the son of Jehoiakim king of Judah were the signet upon my right hand, yet would I pluck thee thence; And I will give thee into the hand of them that seek thy life, and into the hand of them whose face thou fearest, even into the hand of Nebuchadrezzar king of Babylon, and into the hand of the Chaldeans. And I will cast thee out, and thy mother that bare thee, into another country, where ye were not born; and there shall ye die. But to the land whereunto they desire to return, thither shall they not return. Is this man Coniah a despised broken idol? is he a vessel wherein is no pleasure? wherefore are they cast out, he and his seed, and are cast into a land which they know not? O earth, earth, earth, hear the word of the LORD. Thus saith the LORD, Write ye this man childless, a man that shall not prosper in his days: for no man of his seed shall prosper, sitting upon the

throne of David, and ruling any more in Judah. Jeremiah 22:18-30

From the foregoing, we can see that evil records must be erased and the effects of such evil records must be nullified.

PRAYER POINTS

1. *Father God, You said You will be gracious to whom You will be gracious, today, be gracious unto me and deliver me from satanic hold upon my spiritual and physical advancement, in the name of Jesus.*

2. *Father God, You said You will have mercy on whom You will have mercy, be merciful unto me today and completely erase all evil records in my foundation that are troubling my life, in Jesus' name.*

3. I come against all evil records in my foundation, with the resurrection power of the Lord Jesus.

4. I hold the blood of Jesus against recorded ancestral sins holding my breakthroughs in bondage, in the name of Jesus

5. I hold the blood of Jesus against recorded ancestral covenants denying me my divine position in life, in the name of Jesus.

6. I hold the blood of Jesus against every demon assigned to afflict my destiny with 'lepers anointing', because of evil records in my foundation, in the name of Jesus.

7. Evil assignment programmed into the earth to make me a nonentity, come out and die! in the name of Jesus.

8. *By the authority of Calvary, I withdraw all evil pronouncements registered by the sun, the moon and the stars against my advancement, in the name of Jesus.*

9. *By the blood of Jesus, I cancel every witchcraft curse projected into the heavens against my life, in the name of Jesus.*

10. *Hindrances in my spiritual and physical life, coming as a result of the sins of my ancestors, give way by the blood of Jesus!*

11. *Let the thunder of God, scatter every warfare coming against my life from inside the water, river or sea, in the name of Jesus.*

12. *Every curse registered in the circle of the moon, afflicting my health, be nullified by the blood of Jesus!*

13. Every curse registered in the circle of the moon, afflicting my child bearing potentials, be nullified by the blood of Jesus!

14. Every curse registered in the circle of a period, afflicting my marital destiny, be nullified by the blood of Jesus!

15. Every curse registered in the circle of a period, afflicting my glory, be nullified by the blood of Jesus!

16. I stand on the authority of Calvary, and I command every affliction generated against my life from any witchcraft coven and registered in the cycle of a season, to be destroyed now! in Jesus' name.

17. I revoke with the blood of Jesus, every ancestral covenant that gives legal ground to any ancestral spirit to pursue destructive agenda against my life, in the name of Jesus.

18. *Glory of God, overshadow my life and release me from every demonic hold, in the name of Jesus.*

19. *Let the blood of Jesus, nullify every record of untimely death against me, in the name of Jesus*

20. *Wicked practises, recorded in the heavenlies against my family lineage, now affecting my life, be erased by the blood of Jesus and release me!*

Begin to thank God for answering your prayers.

WAR
AGAINST
ANXIETY DEMONS

"When Something bad happens, some people would first of all transfer it to themselves. It is the work of anxiety demons."

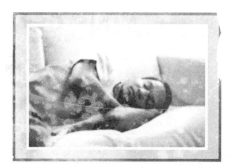

Chapter Four

WAR AGAINST ANXIETY DEMONS

"Cease from anger, and forsake **wrath. Fret not thyself** in any wise to do evil." **This is** simply saying, "Don't let your **anxiety drive** you to a point where you will **sin against** God." Psalm 37:8

"Heaviness in the heart of man **maketh it** stoop; but a good word maketh it **glad." This** is saying that the spirit of anxiety **would turn** a man upside down." Proverbs **12:25**

"Therefore I say unto you, Take no **thought** for your life, what ye shall eat, or **what ye** shall drink; nor yet for your body, **what ye**

shall put on. Is not the life more than meat, and the body than raiment? Behold the fowls of the air. For they sow not, neither do they reap, nor gather into barns; yet your heavenly Father feedeth them. Are ye not much better than they? Which of you by taking thought can add one cubit unto his stature; and why take ye thought for raiment? Consider the lilies of the field, how they grow; they toil not, neither do they spin. And yet I say unto you, that even Solomon in all his glory was not arrayed like one of these. Wherefore, if God so clothe the grass of the field, which today is, and tomorrow is cast into the oven, shall he not much more clothe you, O ye of little faith? Therefore, take no thought, saying, What shall we eat or wherewithal shall we be clothed. For after all these things do the Gentiles seek. For your heavenly Father knoweth that ye have need of all these things. But seek ye first the kingdom of God, and his righteousness; and all these things shall be added unto you. Take therefore no thought for the morrow; for the morrow shall take thought for the things of itself. Sufficient unto the day is the evil thereof." **Matthew 6:25-34**

What is Jesus saying here? He is saying that we should not be anxious about anything:

 "Be careful for nothing, but in everything by prayer and supplication, with thanksgiving let your requests be made known unto God. And the peace of God, which passeth all understanding, shall keep your hearts and minds through Christ Jesus." Philippians 4:6-7

It is when you are not worried, and you go to God in prayer and supplication, that what is written in verse 7 would happen.

If you are a good reader of the Bible, you would have discovered that the vocabulary of God is different from that of man. Many things exist in the physical realm that carry no weight as far as the spiritual realm is concerned. For example, the calendar of January to December exists only here on earth, and so, time exists only here. Means of transportation from one place to another are needed only on earth. In fact, when you read your Bible very well, you can identify five kinds of languages:

1. **The language of God:** When God speaks, He does so with absolute authority and with power. He also speaks with absolute glory. When He speaks, He speaks with absolute might and He speaks with faith and love.

2. **The language of angels:** When an angel is talking, his words are filled with delegated power from God. For example, Angel Gabriel stood and said authoritatively: **"I am Gabriel standing by the altar of God. I have been sent to deliver this message."** Angels have no time or words to waste. They are specific and direct and their words are filled with absolute obedience and commitment to God. Read your Bible very well and you will find that those who asked angels for their names never got an answer.

3. **The language of the natural man:** The language of the natural man is filled with death, sickness, doubt, poverty, hopelessness, fear, confusion, chronic unbelief, hatred, envy and negativity. Sin is the language of the natural man.

    The language of spirit-filled believers: The language of spirit-filled believers is filled with God, faith, power, authority, love and holiness.

5. **The language of the devil:** The language of the devil is filled with lies, deception, woes and destruction. Death is a word from the bottom of hell fire.

It is only in the vocabulary of men that you find words like impossibility, failure and death. In fact, somebody told Jesus that somebody was dead and Jesus said that the person was sleeping. It is in the vocabulary of men that you find poverty, bad luck and defeat. This is why we must readjust our vocabulary. Many of us have been naturally programmed to speak the language of the natural man and the devil. The more we speak these, the more unfavourable the situation becomes.

Examine what you say in the light of the Scripture. The language of God is the language we should be speaking and not the language of the devil. However, we speak the language of defeat because of anxiety spirits.

ANXIETY SPIRITS

Anxiety spirits are very dangerous spirits. Jesus spent time explaining why we should not give them room. Why are these spirits dangerous? It is because a 100 years of worry will not pay one kobo or one dollar debt that you owe. You cry everyday because things are not moving; your tears will not move those things because; crying out of worry does not move God. Worry will not remove tomorrow's problem, it will only deplete your strength for today.

That was why Jesus said: **"Sufficient unto the day is the evil thereof."** Don't carry it to the next day. When tomorrow's burden is added to that of today, it becomes a very heavy load and when a person becomes overloaded, he starts forgetting God and God would become a spectator. Then small problems would look big.

Worry is the interest you pay in advance before the interest is due. Worry will keep a person very busy, but it won't get him anywhere. Those living in worry invite quick death. Worry sends more people to the hospital than all the sicknesses that can be mentioned. Worry kills more people than hard work. A closer look at the origin of the word 'worry' reveals some interesting truths. One source says that it is a division of the mind. Another source says that the word means to strangle or to choke and these are the things that worry do. Worry is very sinful. It produces fear. It is a disease and if a person has it, all other problems come in. A person who is worrying is borrowing a problem that cannot be paid back.

THE GRAVE DIGGER

Worry is a grave digger, it has no sympathy. It kills prematurely and makes people to commit suicide. So, it is a terrible and clever spirit. For example, as you are reading this book, you may be worried but people would not know. You may be smiling but worrying inside. It is not like the sin of adultery, fornication or stealing which can be easily detected.

Worry and anxiety spirits work quietly like termites, eating away mens' souls. It anticipates the trouble which may not really come. For example, when an employer says that he is going to lay off some of his workers, immediately, something would grip the hearts of the worrisome ones who would assume that their names would be included. When eventually the list comes out and their names are not there, all the periods they had spent worrying themselves to death would have been periods of exercise in foolishness because; worry is a very foolish activity.

A person who worries lives like an orphan; without a heavenly Father. If you have a heavenly Father and you know that all things belong to Him, you won't bother yourself at all about anything. Worry is a disgrace to God and a wasted time and effort. It does a lot of havoc to peoples' minds. It is a very clever spirit which moves along with a junior brother called fear. Immediately worry comes in, fear is standing at the door and when the two move in, Mr. Discouragement will also move in and the victim would be finished.

A KINGDOM

As you are now, you are a whole entity by yourself. Individually, you are a kingdom, you are a house, a spirit, you are living in a body and you have a soul. Whatever your name is called, the real you is your spirit. Your soul and body are your tools for functioning as a human being on earth. As a Christian, when you die, your physical body will be discarded and replaced by the resurrection body of Jesus.

The soul and the spirit man either go to heaven or hell fire because the spirit and soul go together. God's proper order is that your body should be in submission to your soul, and your soul should be in submission to your spirit, then the whole man should be in submission to God. However, when worry steps in, it creates disorder and the mind will be jumping from one place to another.

A person who is trying to pray and at the same time is thinking about how bad the situation is can never be fervent in prayer. This is the most terrible thing about worry. It sucks the blood of prayer, this is why we must really deal with it.

At a particular psychiatric hospital, before a patient is discharged, a small test is carried out on him. They would push the patient into a room, open a tap and give him a mop. If he goes to the tap and closes it, they would know that he is well, but 90 percent of the patients would not close the tap. They would continue to mop the water while the tap is left open and some continue like that until they collapse out of exhaustion. Many people are like that. They take the mop of crying, grumbling, fighting, shouting, drinking, dancing, socialising or music, while the tap of anxiety is still opened.

What we need to do is to bind and cast out anxiety spirits. When they are controlling a person, the person may be feeling headache and may take all kinds of drugs, but the headache will not go. Anxiety spirits also cause pain in the neck, restlessness, etc.

A man prayed to God for blessing and God blessed him so much that he had ten transportation vehicles. Every night, he was at the gate watching them coming in one after the other. If any of them took time in coming in, he would start pacing up and down, worrying about what might have happened to it. He would be afraid that it might have been involved in an accident or that the police might have arrested its driver. This way, he doubted the power of the God that blessed him.

UNHEALTHY ANXIETY

When something bad happens, some people would first of all transfer it to themselves. It is the work of anxiety demons. When some people are troubled, you would see their hands trembling. At that moment, they cannot hold anything or see clearly. When some people are attacked by anxiety demons, they feel tired. You know that you are not tired but something is telling you that you are tired, it is an anxiety demon at work.

Sometimes, the attack results in dryness of the mouth or loss of appetite. This demon can also cause some people to have diarrhea. You may think that what you have is a big problem, but perhaps all you need do is to go and close the tap instead of using the mop and running all over the place. All the lightheadedness and uneasy feelings are the handwork of demons of anxiety. Intense or irrational fear and emotional stress are also evidence that a demon of anxiety is at work.

A sister complained that all the seven men who proposed marriage to her disappointed her and she drew the conclusion that all men are wicked. When the eighth man came, she said: "This one may probably behave like the rest so I will place him on trial." The man said that he did not want to be placed on trial. What happened was that anxiety demons have taken over. These clever spirits come in when miracles are piled up and very slowly and gently leak them out. You really need to deal with them!

The Lord has a lot to do for you if you would cast all your cares on Jesus and stop carrying them by yourself. Release everything into His holy hands, then pray your normal prayers and read your Bible. You will be shocked at what the Lord will do for you. Many people need deliverance from these spirits. Sometimes, when these spirits have entered into a life, hypertension, diabetes and all kinds of things come in, but once you close the tap and say: "Look Satan, I am not going to worry my brain about anything because the Bible says: **"Be careful for nothing"**, you will be released.

THE BANE OF INSOMNIA

Some people constantly feel that something bad is going to happen to them. I saw somebody going from place to place in search of help because he honestly believed that he had H.I.V. He went for a test and it was negative. He came back and said, "No, I must go to another place." I asked him why he was doing that and he said, "It is because I read a book on it and everything they say would happen in the book is happening to me." That was anxiety demon at work.

A lot of people fear for their safety, fear for their family, their friends and fear for losing control of their affairs. Some are highly irritable; if any small thing happens to them, they would explode. They get easily frustrated. They find it difficult to sleep and when they wake up, they are unable to sleep again or they are frightened in their dreams. Some exercise the fear of going mad. All these are anxiety demons at work.

Some are worried that they may not find a husband; when they find a husband, they are worried that he may run away. Some are worried that they don't have money; when they have money, they are afraid that it would not last. Some are praying for God to send them abroad and when God sends them abroad, they would be shaking inside the plane. They are afraid that the plane may crash land - that is anxiety spirit at work! It is the elder brother of fear and discouragement is close to it.

THE WAY OUT

The most important thing to do is to repent. Worry is a sin, so ask the Lord to forgive you.

PRAYER POINTS

1. *Every evil power that anxiety has introduced into my life, come out now! in the name of Jesus.*

2. *You demon of fear, come out with your entire root, in the name of Jesus.*

3. *I return every witchcraft curse back to the sender, in the name of Jesus.*

4. *The enemy will not drag my life on the ground, in the name of Jesus.*

5. *Every fear of financial failure, vanish! in the name of Jesus.*

6. *Every satanic load in my spirit, go back to your sender! in the name of Jesus.*

7. *Every body of water harbouring my blessings, release them now! in the name of Jesus.*

8. *Every witchcraft operation against my prosperity, be dismantled by fire! in the name of Jesus.*

9. *Every satanic prayer issued against me, be nullified! in the name of Jesus.*

10. *You my business, multiply! in the name of Jesus.*

11. *O Lord, let no man prevail against me, in the name of Jesus.*

12. *I bind every spirit of anxiety and I cast them out, in the name of Jesus.*

13. *(Lay your hand on your chest): Every internal cage, be broken to pieces! in the name of Jesus.*

OTHER BOOKS BY DR. D. K. OLUKOYA

1. 20 Marching Orders To Fulfil Your Destiny
2. 30 Things The Anointing Can Do For You
3. 30 Poverty Destroying Keys
4. 30 Prophetic Arrows From Heaven
5. A-Z of Complete Deliverance
6. Abraham's Children in Bondage
7. Basic Prayer Patterns
8. Be Prepared
9. Bewitchment must Die
10. Biblical Principles of Dream Interpretation
11. Biblical Principles of Long Life
12. Born Great, But Tied Down
13. Breaking Bad Habits
14. Breakthrough Prayers For Business Professionals
15. Bringing Down The Power of God
16. Brokenness
17. Can God Trust You?
18. Can God?
19. Command The Morning
20. Connecting to The God of Breakthroughs

OTHER BOOKS BY DR. D. K. OLUKOYA

OTHER BOOKS BY DR. D. K. OLUKOYA

41. Deliverance of The Brain
42. Deliverance Of The Conscience
43. Deliverance By Fire
44. Destiny Clinic
45. Destroying Satanic Masks
46. Disgracing Soul Hunters
47. Divine Yellow Card
48. Divine Prescription For Your Total Immunity
49. Divine Military Training
50. Dominion Prosperity
51. Drawers Of Power From The Heavenlies
52. Evil Appetite
53. Evil Umbrella
54. Facing Both Ways
55. Failure In The School Of Prayer
56. Fire For Life's Journey
57. Fire for Spiritual Battles for The 21st Century Army
58. For We Wrestle...
59. Freedom Indeed
60. Fresh Fire (Bilingual book in French)

OTHER BOOKS BY DR. D. K. OLUKOYA

OTHER BOOKS BY DR. D. K. OLUKOYA

OTHER BOOKS BY DR. D. K. OLUKOYA

OTHER BOOKS BY DR. D. K. OLUKOYA

OTHER BOOKS BY DR. D. K. OLUKOYA

OTHER BOOKS BY DR. D. K. OLUKOYA

159. The Chain Breaker
160. The Dining Table of Darkness
161. The Enemy Has Done This
162. The Evil Cry Of Your Family Idol
163. The Fire of Revival
164. The School of Tribulation
165. The Gateway To Spiritual Power
166. The Great Deliverance
167. The Internal Stumbling Block
168. The Lord Is A Man Of War
169. The Mystery Of Mobile Curses
170. The Mystery Of The Mobile Temple
171. The Prayer Eagle
172. The University of Champions
173. The Power of Aggressive Prayer Warriors
174. The Power of Priority
175. The Tongue Trap
176. The Terrible Agenda
177. The Scale of The Almighty
178. The Hidden Viper

OTHER BOOKS BY DR. D. K. OLUKOYA

OTHER BOOKS BY DR. D. K. OLUKOYA

YORUBA PUBLICATION

1. Adúrà Agbàyọrî
2. Adúrà Tî Nṣî Òkè Nî'dîi
3. Òjò Adúrà

FRENCH PUBLICATIONS

1. Pluire De Prière
2. Espirit De Vagabondage
3. En Finir Avec Les Forces Maléfiques De La Maison De Ton Pére
4. Que l'envoutement Périsse
5. Frappez I'adversaire Et Il Fuira
6. Comment Recevior La Délivrance Du Mari Et De La Femme De Nuit
7. Comment Se Délivrer Soi-mếme
8. Pouvoir Contre Les Terrorites Spirituels
9. Prière De Percées Pour Les Hommes D'affaires
10. Prier Jusqu'à Remporter La Victoire
11. Prières Violentes Pour Humilier Les Problèmes Opiniâtres
12. Prière Pour Détruire Les Maladies Et Les Infirmités

34.   L'etoile Dans Votre Ciel

35.   Les Saisons De La Vie

36.   Femme Tu Es Liberee

ANNUAL 70 DAYS PRAYER AND FASTING PUBLICATIONS

1.   Prayers That Bring Miracles

2.   Let God Answer By Fire

3.   Prayers To Mount With Wings As Eagles

4.   Prayers That Bring Explosive Increase

5.   Prayers For Open Heavens

6.   Prayers To Make You Fulfil Your Divine Destiny

7.   Prayers That Make God To Answer And Fight By Fire

8.   Prayers That Bring Unchallengeable Victory and Breakthrough Rainfall Bombardments

9.   Prayers That Bring Dominion Prosperity And Uncommon Success

10. Prayers That Bring Power and Overflowing Progress

11. Prayers That Bring Laughter And Enlargement Breakthroughs

12. Prayers That Bring Uncommon Favour And Breakthroughs

13. Prayers That Bring Unprecendented Greatness & Unmatchable Increase

14. Prayers That Bring Awesome Testimonies And Turn Around Breakthroughs.

THIS BOOK AND MORE ARE OBTAINABLE AT:

* MFM Press & Bookstores
54, Akeju Street, Off Shipeolu Street, Onipanu, Lagos.
Contact: 018144074, 08028127811.
MFM Press Prayer City Branch
1st Floor, Modern Shopping Mall, MFM Prayer City
Km. 12, Lagos Ibadan Exp. Way, Ibafo, Ogun State.
Contact: 08060784128

* MFM International Bookshop
13, Olasimbo Street, Off Olumo Str., Onike, Yaba.

* The Battle Cry Christian Ministries
322, Herbert Macaulay Way, Sabo, Yaba, Lagos.

* IPFY Music Konnections Limited
48, Opebi Road, Salvation Bus Stop
Contact: 234-1-4719471, 234-8033056093

* All MFM Church branches nationwide and Christian bookstores.